The Bible fact or fairytale

....

Marilyn Downs

Downs Literature

Copyright © 2025 by Marilyn Downs

All rights reserved.

No portion of this book may be reproduced in any form without written permission from the publisher or author, except as permitted by U.S. copyright law.

Contents

Intro	1
1. In the Beginning?	2
2. Was There a Garden?	12
3. A Little Rain	17
4. Fire from Heaven	23
5. Exiled	28
6. The Blood that Speaks	35
7. Science and the Bible	42
8. King or Prophet	46
9. Integrating Science and Faith	51
10. The Death of Jesus	58
11. Was There a Ressurection	65
12. The Nephilim and the Kandahar Giant	72
13. Ascension	78
14. Conclusion: A Path Forward	84
References	91

Intro

This book explores human history and scientific discoveries in relation to the Bible. It does not seek to dictate what you should believe; rather, it serves as a tool to help you form your own conclusions. Within these pages, you will encounter both evidence and interpretation.

Chapter One

In the Beginning?

How Old is the Earth

This chapter explores one of humans oldest and most debated questions: How old is the Earth? We'll examine scientific research and biblical interpretation, allowing you to weigh the evidence and form your own beliefs.

How Old Is the Earth According to Science

the oldest rocks on Earth

Zircon Dating

Zircon crystals are ideal for radiometric dating. When they form, zircon crystals naturally contain uranium but exclude lead. Measuring uranium and lead isotopes in zircon gives precise age estimates for ancient rocks.

Meteorite Dating:

Meteorites are considered "time capsules" from the early solar system. Dating them also gives us a strong estimate of the Earth's age.

Scientific Conclusion:

Based on these methods, scientists estimate that the Earth is approximately 4.54 billion years old. Data from meteorites, moon rocks, and Earth's geological formations support this estimate. Proof News AI Project. https://www.groovy-geologist.com/ai.html

How Old Is the Earth According to the Bible?

Many who study the Bible turn to the genealogies in Genesis, particularly chapters 5 and 11, to estimate the age of the Earth. These genealogies trace a timeline from Adam to Noah and then from Noah to Abraham.

Using these records, some scholars calculate the age of the Earth to be around 6,000 to 10,000 years. This belief is commonly known as Young Earth Creationism.

Key Beliefs of Young Earth Creationism:
- The six days of creation in Genesis 1 are interpreted as literal 24-hour days.
- The genealogies are considered complete, allowing for an unbroken timeline back to the beginning. Earth was created directly by God in a short period, not over billions of years.

Alternative Christian Interpretations: Not all Christians take the six day creation story literally. Some see it as poetic or symbolic, with each "day" possibly representing an age or era. This view facilitates reconciliation between Scripture and scientific estimates of the Earth's age.

Could Both Be Right?

Someone once said there is no time in heaven, that heaven is eternity. If that's true, could it be that God's timeline is completely different from ours?

It's hard to understand. We live by clocks, calendars, and aging bodies, but God—the Creator of time—is not limited by them.

To Him, the beginning, the end, and everything in between are visible and accessible simultaneously. What seems contradictory may be truth from a different dimension—a reality we can't fully grasp yet.

Both answers may be accurate. The Earth is ancient, as evidenced by scientific findings. The Bible's timeline is accurate in the context of a timeless God who views history not as a linear progression but as a unified whole.

Is the Earth Flat or Round?

Modern science is precise: the Earth is an oblate spheroid—a slightly flattened sphere. However, some have questioned this throughout history, and even today, the flat Earth theory persists among small groups.

Let's look at the evidence.

Visual Observations
- Ships gradually disappear hull-first over the horizon.

- The Earth casts a round shadow on the Moon during a lunar eclipse. https://almanahj.com/us/id=2251

Space Exploration

Astronauts have captured photos of Earth from orbit and the Moon, showing the Earth as a round planet.

Geodetic Surveys

Earth's curvature is consistently measured using satellites and ground-based instruments.

Celestial Patterns

The movement of stars and the Sun only makes sense on a spherical Earth.

Conclusion:

The evidence for a round Earth is overwhelming. Flat Earth theories have been repeatedly debunked and are not supported by any credible scientific body.

Who Wrote the Bible?

The Bible is sacred for Christians, Jews, Samaritans, and others. It contains many books written by many people over over a thousand years.

The Old Testament (Hebrew Bible)

Prophets, poets, and historians wrote these texts. Some names are known—like Moses, David, and Isaiah—but many authors remain anonymous. These books were written over centuries, edited, and passed down through generations. The

New Testament Focused on the life, death, and resurrection of Jesus, this section includes:

- The Gospels (Matthew, Mark, Luke, and John)
- The Acts of the Apostles
- Epistles (letters) from Paul, Peter, James, and others
- Revelation

These texts were written in the 1st century A.D. by Jesus' early followers.

Inspired or Man Made?

Many believe the Bible was written under divine inspiration, meaning God worked through people to convey His message. Others consider it a deeply human effort to record spiritual experiences, traditions, and moral teachings.

Regardless of how one views it, the Bible is the most printed, read, and translated book in history.

The Bible contains hundreds of prophecies, many of which believers claim have been fulfilled with historical accuracy. This section presents a selection of well-known prophecies, followed by the events corresponding to their fulfillment. Whether you approach these texts from a faith-based perspective or a historical curiosity, the overlap between biblical predictions and recorded events is undeniably compelling.
https://www.chaplainscollegeschoolofgraduatestudies.com/chapel-blog/poof-that-the-bible-is-the-word-of-god

1. Isaiah 7:14 – The Virgin Birth

Prophecy:

Isaiah foretells, "Therefore the Lord himself will give you a sign: The virgin will conceive and give birth to a son and will call him Immanuel."

Fulfillment:

Christians see the birth of Jesus as the fulfillment of this prophecy. Christ, who was born of the Virgin Mary. Matthew 1:22–23 references this directly, presenting Jesus as the Immanuel, or "God with us."

2. Micah 5:2 – The Messiah's Birthplace

Prophecy

Micah declares that the ruler of Israel would come from Bethlehem: "But you, Bethlehem Ephrathah, though you are small... out of you will come for me one who will be ruler over Israel."

Fulfillment:

According to the Gospels, Jesus was born in Bethlehem, fulfilling this ancient prophecy (Luke 2:4–7).

3. Isaiah 53 – The Suffering Servant

Prophecy:

Isaiah describes a servant who would be "pierced for our transgressions" and bear the punishment of others. This figure suffers silently, is despised, and is rejected.

Fulfillment:

Christians believe this was fulfilled in Jesus' crucifixion. The Gospel of John and other New Testament texts describe Jesus' suffering in language that closely mirrors the prophecy of Isaiah.

4. Psalm 22 – The Crucifixion Foreshadowed

Prophecy:

King David writes, "They pierce my hands and my feet" and "Divide my clothes among them and cast lots for my garment."

Fulfillment:

Jesus quotes this Psalm on the cross, saying, "My God, my God, why have you forsaken me?" (Matthew 27:46). The physical details—piercing of hands and feet, casting lots for his clothing—are seen by many as a prophetic preview of the crucifixion, which took place centuries after Psalm 22 was written.

5. Ezekiel 26 – The Fall of Tyre

Prophecy:

Ezekiel predicts the destruction of Tyre. He says it will be scraped bare like a rock and its debris thrown into the sea.

Fulfillment:

Nebuchadnezzar besieged Tyre, which was later destroyed by Alexander the Great, who used its rubble to build a causeway to the island part of the city. The prophecy's detail about debris being thrown into the sea was unexpectedly fulfilled during that event.

6. Isaiah 13:19–22 – The Fall of Babylon

Prophecy:

Babylon, the jewel of kingdoms, would be overthrown like Sodom and Gomorrah and never inhabited again.

Fulfillment:

The Persians eventually conquered Babylon and subsequently brought it to ruin. Although some inhabitants lived nearby, the central city was abandoned and has never been rebuilt as a thriving metropolis.

7. Deuteronomy 28:64 – The Scattering of Israel

Prophecy:

Moses warns that disobedience would result in the scattering of the Israelites across the nations.

Fulfillment:

Following the destruction of the Second Temple in A.D. 70, the Jewish people were dispersed throughout the world—a historical event often called the Jewish Diaspora.

8. Ezekiel 37:21–22 – The Regathering of Israel

Prophecy:

God promises to regather the Israelites from among the nations and bring them back into their land to become one nation again.

Fulfillment:

In 1948, Israel was officially declared a nation. Many Christians and Jewish scholars view this as a direct fulfillment of Ezekiel's prophecy, especially given the centuries of exile. Takeaways from Israel! https://www.thebasicswithbeth.com/blog/takeaways-from-israel

9. Daniel 2 – The Rise and Fall of Empires

Prophecy:

Daniel interprets a dream given to King Nebuchadnezzar. The dream depicts a statue crafted from various metals, each representing successive empires: Babylon, Medo-Persia, Greece, and Rome.

Fulfillment:

Historians agree that these four empires rose and fell in the order described. The accuracy of the sequence has led both religious and secular scholars to marvel at Daniel's foresight—or, as some critics suggest, retrospective narrative.

10. Matthew 24:1–2 – The Destruction of the Temple

Prophecy:

Jesus predicts that the Jewish Temple will be utterly destroyed, with "not one stone left upon another."

Fulfillment:
In A.D. 70, Roman forces under Titus destroyed Jerusalem and the Second Temple. The structure was torn down, fulfilling Jesus' exact prediction.

These ten examples represent just a portion of the many prophetic statements in the Bible. Whether interpreted as divine insight or a remarkable historical coincidence, these prophecies have profoundly influenced the faith of millions. They continue to inspire study, debate, and reflection—especially in light of future prophecies yet to be fulfilled.

Skeptical Counterpoints Skeptics argue that:

Some "fulfilled" prophecies may be vague or open to interpretation.

Specific prophecies might have been written or edited after the events occurred.

Events like Israel's rebirth could be attributed to human political movements rather than divine intervention.

Self-fulfilling prophecies (like Jesus deliberately doing things to align with prophecy) could play a role.

The Logical Leap: Faith or Fact?

It So, is it logical to conclude that the Bible is true and inspired by God because of fulfilled prophecy?

From a believer's standpoint—yes. Prophecy is one of the most powerful theological tools used to support the divine authorship of Scripture.

However, for someone skeptical or secular—it may not be definitive proof. Matthew 1-2: The birth of the Christ. – Twenty-Eight Eighteen. https://twentyeighteighteen.com/2015/01/10/matthew-1-2-the-birth-of-the-christ/

"While interpretations may vary, the volume and specificity of fulfilled prophecies in the Bible invite us to pause. Is this the product of chance—or a divine hand? To many, it seems logical that a book with such predictive power is not merely historical, but holy."

Chapter Two

Was There a Garden?

From a scientific perspective, the story of the Garden of Eden is regarded as a religious myth rather than a historical or scientific account. The narrative is not supported by scientific evidence and is understood within the context of religious belief and cultural tradition

Science focuses on empirical evidence, observation, experimentation, and the natural world to understand phenomena. The story of the Garden of Eden, with its supernatural elements and theological symbolism, falls outside the scope of scientific inquiry.

From a historical and archaeological standpoint, no evidence supports the existence of a literal Garden of Eden as described in religious texts. The concept of a pristine paradise with specific geographical features and supernatural beings is not substantiated by archaeological findings or historical records.

The narrative of the Garden of Eden raises questions that are not within the purview of scientific investigation, such as the existence of divine beings, the nature of sin, and the consequences of human disobedience.

While the Garden of Eden story holds profound religious and cultural significance for many people, its interpretation and understanding are matters of faith and theology rather than empirical science. As such, it is not within the domain of science to validate or refute religious narratives like the Garden of Eden.

One could argue scientific fact, based on NDE "near death experience", There are a small percentage of doctors who do believe in NDE's, due to professional experiences with patients that defy all odds.

That being said, people who have claimed to visit through an NDE claimed to have seen the Garden of Eden in heaven,

What happened in the Garden of Eden?

The Garden of Eden story is a fundamental narrative in Abrahamic religions, particularly Judaism, Christianity, and Islam. It is primarily found in the book of Genesis in the Hebrew Bible (Old Testament) and the Quran. The story is rich in symbolism and theological significance, and interpretations may vary among different religious traditions.

Here's a summary of the story as presented in Genesis:

Creation of Adam and Eve:

According to the Genesis account, God created the first human, Adam, from the dust of the ground and breathed life into him. God then placed Adam in the Garden of Eden, a paradise filled with lush vegetation, rivers, and trees bearing fruit. God commands Adam to cultivate and care for the garden.

Forbidden Fruit:

Amid the garden, God plants the tree of the knowledge of good and evil and instructs Adam not to eat from its fruit, warning that doing so will result in death.

Temptation and Fall:

God creates Eve, the first woman, from one of Adam's ribs to be his companion. They live together in harmony in the garden until they encounter the serpent, traditionally identified with Satan or the devil. The serpent tempts Eve to eat the fruit from the forbidden tree, questioning God's command and suggesting that eating the fruit will make her like God, knowing good and evil. Eve succumbs to the temptation and eats the fruit, and she also gives some to Adam, who eats it as well.

Consequences:

enjoyed, experiencing hardship, suffering, and mortality.

The story of the Garden of Eden is interpreted in various ways. It symbolizes themes such as the origin of sin, the consequences of disobedience, the loss of innocence, and humanity's ongoing struggle between good and evil. It serves as a foundational myth.

The Search for Eden: Clues from the Rivers

The Bible describes the Garden of Eden as not just a paradise but a real geographical place with rivers flowing through and out of it. Genesis 2:10–14 mentions a river that flowed out of Eden and divided into four headwaters: Pishon, Gihon, Tigris, and Euphrates. The Tigris and Euphrates are still known today, flowing through modern-day Iraq.

This detail has led many to believe that the Garden of Eden may have once been located in the region historically known as Mesopotamia, meaning "land between the rivers." This area, often called the "Cradle of Civilization," includes parts of modern Iraq, Syria, Iran, and Turkey.

The challenge lies in the other two rivers—Pishon and Gihon, which are harder to identify. Some scholars and explorers believe the Pishon might correspond to a now-dry riverbed called the Wadi Batin or an ancient river once flowing through the Arabian Peninsula. Others associate the Gihon with the Nile or an ancient river in the region of Cush, possibly located in northeast Africa.

Satellite imagery has even revealed evidence of ancient river channels buried under desert sands, supporting the possibility that Eden was a literal place now obscured by time, climate change, or even catastrophe.

Of course, there's also the argument that Eden no longer exists in our physical realm—some believe it was removed or destroyed after the fall of man, becoming a spiritual or symbolic location rather than one we can dig up and map.

Still, the geographical clues in Genesis continue to intrigue historians, archaeologists, and believers alike. If Eden was honest, its rivers might still whisper its secrets—waiting for discovery, or perhaps meant only as a signpost pointing us back to a perfect beginning lost to time.

Chapter Three

A Little Rain

The story of Noah's Ark is one of the most enduring—and debated—accounts in the Bible. Was it just a moral tale, or did it happen?

This chapter explores the biblical flood account, the construction and scale of the ark, and some of the modern claims and controversies surrounding it.

What Were the Dimensions of the Ark?

."This is how you are to build it: The ark is to be three hundred cubits long, fifty cubits wide, and thirty cubits high."

A cubit is commonly estimated to be 18 inches (45 cm), although its measurement varies across different cultures.

That would make the ark approximately.

- 450 feet long (137 meters)
    - 75 feet wide (23 meters)
    - 45 feet high (14 meters)

That's longer than a football field and roughly the size of a small cargo ship—massive for its time and, according to some, structurally sound even by modern standards.

How Long Did It Take to Build the Ark?

While the Bible doesn't give a precise construction timeline, we're told:

- Noah was 500 years old when he fathered his sons (Genesis 5:32)

- He was 600 when the flood began (Genesis 7:6)

Historical records suggest that the ark may have taken up to 100 years to build. During that time, Noah obeyed God's command and built the ark despite ridicule, disbelief, and the absence of visible rain.

What Was the Ark Made Of?

Genesis 6:14 instructs Noah to build the ark from gopher wood, a material whose exact identity remains unknown. It was likely a durable wood known in ancient Mesopotamia, such as cedar or cypress.

Noah also coated the ark, both inside and out, with pitch, making it waterproof and resilient. The ark had three decks, multiple rooms, a single door, and a window—it was designed more like a floating survival shelter than a seafaring vessel.

What Happened in the Flood?

Here's a summary of the flood narrative from Genesis 6–9:

- Divine Warning: God sees the wickedness of humanity and decides to send a flood to cleanse the earth. He warns Noah and instructs him to build the ark.

- The Ark Is Built: Noah spent decades constructing it, following God's exact specifications.

- The Rain Begins: Once the ark is finished, Noah, his family, and pairs of animals enter the ark. Then, it rains forty days and nights, and the fountains of the deep burst forth.

- The Earth Floods: Water covers everything—even the highest mountains. All life outside the ark perishes.

- The Waters Recede: After 150 days, the water level begins to decrease. The ark comes to rest on the mountains of Ararat.

- A New Start: Noah and his family exit the ark and repopulate the earth once the ground dries. God places a rainbow in the sky as a sign of the covenant, promising never to destroy the world with a flood again.

Is There Proof of the Ark?

For centuries, explorers and believers have searched for physical evidence of Noah's Ark, Some claims have sparked intense debate and international interest.

Ararat Theories:

Genesis says the ark came to rest on Mount Ararat, located in eastern Turkey. The location is harsh and often inaccessible, but that hasn't stopped explorers from searching.

- The Durupınar Site: This boat-shaped formation near Mount Ararat gained attention in the 1950s and is now a protected site and a Turkish national monument. Some believe it could be petrified remains of an ancient ark, though many scientists argue that it's a natural rock formation.

- Anchor Stones: Massive stone slabs with holes in them—found in the region—have been interpreted by some as ancient drogue stones, used to stabilize ships in turbulent water.

Noah's Tomb?

Several locations, including one in Turkey and another in Lebanon, claim to be the gravesites of Noah, but none have been definitively proven to be so.

Mysterious Metal?

Some reports claim that artificial metal not found in nature was discovered near ark sites, though such claims remain unverified and controversial.

What Do Scientists Say About the Flood?

Mainstream science does not support the concept of a global flood as described in the Genesis account. Here's why:

- Lack of geological evidence for a planet-wide flood covering mountains.

- Fossil records don't show the sudden worldwide extinction of land animals. (although there have been many fossils encountered that are animals in the process of living e.g., a fish in the process of eating another fish, for such a thing to happen, it would have to be a catastrophic event for it to be frozen in place while it was eating fish.)

- Challenges with the logistics of gathering, feeding, and managing animals from every species. (One could argue that the animals that were brought on the ark were babies; it would have made the event more plausible.)

However, many scientists and historians acknowledge that massive regional floods have occurred; such as those in ancient Mesopotamia, where the biblical story is likely to have originated. Some believe that a real, catastrophic flood could have inspired the narrative of Noah.

There's also a surprising overlap between Genesis and ancient flood myths, such as the Epic of Gilgamesh, suggesting a shared memory of a devastating flood in human history.
How Many People Were on Noah's Ark? - Free Bible Study Hub. https://www.freebiblestudyhub.com/archives/6291

Faith and the Flood

Whether you believe the flood happened exactly as described or see it as symbolic, one thing we know for certain is that most areas in the world show that whether the flood was worldwide or localized, remains to be seen.

Chapter Four

Fire from Heaven

What happened in Sodom and Gomorrah? Was it just a moral tale about judgment, or is there actual evidence of divine destruction buried beneath the ash and dust near the Dead Sea? This chapter explores both the biblical account and scientific investigations into one of the Bible's most dramatic events.

What Was Sodom and Gomorrah?

Sodom and Gomorrah were ancient cities mentioned in Genesis, known for extreme wickedness, violence, and corruption. According to Genesis 13:13, "Now the people of Sodom were wicked and were sinning greatly against the Lord." Their reputations became so infamous that "Sodom" is still used today as a symbol of immorality.

God tells Abraham that He plans to destroy the cities, but Abraham intercedes, pleading for mercy if even ten righteous people can be found. Unfortunately, the cities are found to be beyond redemption.

Abraham, Lot, and the Angels

God sends two angels to the city of Sodom, where Abraham's nephew, Lot, takes them in. The men of the city surround Lot's home, demanding to abuse the visitors. Lot pleads with them and tries to protect the guests, who reveal themselves as angels. They strike the men with blindness and warn Lot to flee immediately.

Lot is told to take his family and escape to the mountains, because destruction is imminent. As the sun rises, God rains down fire and brimstone from the heavens.

Lot's Wife?

As Lot and his family flee, they are warned not to look back. But Lot's wife disobeys—she turns and looks at the destruction behind her. Instantly, she is turned into a pillar of salt.

Her story has long been interpreted as a cautionary tale about the consequences of disobedience, regret, and clinging to the past. It's a powerful image: turning back to something God is rescuing you from may cost you everything.

Is It Normal for Sulfur to Be Embedded in Rock?

In natural environments, sulfur is typically found in a yellowish form, mixed with minerals, and is often located near vents or lava fields. But the sulfur found in this region is often:

- Pure white

- Nearly 100% pure sulfur

- Encased in a burned crust

Balls of Sulfur in the Rocks

Explorers and independent researchers have found actual sulfur balls embedded in the ashen terrain near the Dead Sea. These balls:

- Burn at low temperatures

- Leave a sticky, oily residue

- It can still be ignited today

Some believe these sulfur balls are physical evidence of the "fire and brimstone" described in the Book of Genesis. Others argue it's a geological coincidence. Still, the purity and location raise significant questions.

Why Is This Sulfur Different?

The sulfur discovered in this region is:

- Chemically distinct from volcanic sulfur

- Found only in specific burned-out regions

- Surrounded by collapsed, blackened, and ashen material

Could this indicate an ancient supernatural occurrence? Or is it an unknown type of natural disaster?

Were Any Buildings Found?

Some sites near the Dead Sea—including the proposed ruins of Sodom—contain:

- **Burned ruins**

- **Ash-layered walls**

- **Structures resembling ancient buildings**

Archaeologist Dr. Steven Collins and others working at Tall el-Hammam have uncovered city gates, palace-like foundations, and melted bricks. The site was abandoned for hundreds of years after a massive heat event. Could this be biblical Sodom?

Were Any Skeletons Found?

Reports from the Tall el-Hammam excavation suggest that human remains may have been found, fragmented, and damaged by extreme heat. The destruction pattern is similar to what would be seen after a thermal blast—instant, high-heat devastation.

Scientists and biblical archaeologists continue to study the site, debating whether it truly matches the biblical account. But the convergence of ash, melted material, and sulfur-laced rugged terrain is difficult to ignore.

Faith and Fire

Whether you believe in a literal rain of fire from heaven or interpret the story symbolically, the account of Sodom and Gomorrah carries deep spiritual weight.

Chapter Five

Exiled

The story of Moses and the Exodus is one of the most foundational and dramatic accounts in the Bible. It tells of slavery, plagues, miracles, and a nation led from captivity into freedom. But did it happen? Or is it a carefully constructed legend? This chapter explores the faith, the facts, and the friction between them.

Moses

Moses is portrayed as a prophet, liberator, and lawgiver in the Bible. According to Britannica, he flourished in the 14th–13th century BCE and is credited with leading the Hebrews out of Egyptian slavery and forming the nation of Israel at Mount Sinai.

Some scholars see Moses as a real historical figure. Others believe he may be a symbolic composite of several leaders from ancient Hebrew traditions. Regardless, the impact of Moses on world religions and human history is undeniable.

Moses in Egypt

According to the Book of Exodus, Moses, alongside his brother Aaron, confronts Pharaoh to demand the release of the enslaved Hebrews. Pharaoh refuses, leading to a dramatic showdown between human pride and divine power.

Pharaoh's Daughter and the Baby in the Basket

Moses' story begins with an act of rescue. As Pharaoh orders the death of all Hebrew male infants, Moses' mother places him in a basket and sets him adrift on the Nile. Pharaoh's daughter finds the child, takes pity, and raises him as her own in the royal palace.

This origin story is rich in irony: the man chosen to deliver the Hebrews is raised in the very household that enslaved them.

The Plagues of Egypt

The Ten Plagues—blood, frogs, gnats, boils, darkness, and the death of the firstborn—are described as divine judgments against Egypt's false gods and hardened hearts.

Some scientists and historians have proposed naturalistic explanations:

- Red algae or "red tide" turning the water to blood

- Volcanic ash causing darkness

- Disease and ecological chain reactions causing livestock death and human illness

But others argue that the precise timing, intensity, and cumulative effect of the plagues go beyond coincidence, and point to something supernatural. Furthermore, who is to say that God did not use these natural phenomena to do his work?

The Hebrews' Exile

The Exodus is described as a mass migration of hundreds of thousands of Hebrews from Egypt into the wilderness. Some scholars argue this number may be exaggerated or symbolic, while others suggest the migration could have involved a smaller group with a significant cultural impact.

Archaeological evidence of such a significant movement is scarce. However, some believe this is due to the transient, nomadic nature of the journey and the shifting sands of time.

At this point, to excavate anything on the Saudi Arabian side, archaeologists would be shot on site. For years people have tried to excavate chariot wheels out of the Red Sea, but as of current days, they have been unsuccessful due to Saudi Arabian law.

Here is a link to some pictures taken under the Red Sea:
   https://www.envisionbibleworld.com/2018/04/chariot-wheels-found-red-sea/

There's a video on Reddit that maps out what is believed to be the true Exodus in the Red Sea and Saudi Arabia.

This is a link to his video.

https://www.reddit.com/r/HighStrangeness/comments/1ahz1dg/did_ron_wyatt_discover_the_red_sea_crossing/?utm_source=share&utm_medium=web3x&utm_name=web3xcss&utm_term=1&utm_content=share_butt

The Parting of the Red Sea

Perhaps the most cinematic moment in the Exodus story is the parting of the sea.

As the Israelites flee, God parts the waters, allowing them to walk through on dry ground. The pursuing Egyptian army is swallowed by the returning waves.

Special archaeological dives have taken place, and a giant shelf, like a pathway, was discovered all the way across the Red Sea between Egypt and Saudi Arabia.

Some researchers argue that the "Red Sea" may have been a mistranslation of "Reed Sea"—a shallow marsh. Others suggest the Gulf of Aqaba is the real crossing point, where some claim to have found coral-covered chariot wheels on the sea floor.

paizo.com - Forums: Off-Topic Discussions: A Civil Religious Discussion. https://paizo.com/threads/rzs2h9ei&page=128?A-Civil-Religious-Discussion

There's a video on the internet that shows a man mapping out what he believes to be proof of discoveries in the Red Sea and in Saudi Arabia from archaeologists.

This is a link to his video.

https://www.reddit.com/r/HighStrangeness/comments/1ahz1dg/did_ron_wyatt_di

scover_the_red_sea_crossing/?utm_source=share&utm_medium=web3x&utm_name=web3xcss&utm_term=1&utm_content=share_butt

> Here's another video that claims to be proof of the crossing of the Red Sea.
> https://www.tiktok.com/t/ZP8ryerXX/

Mount Sinai and the Ten Commandments

After the Exodus, the Israelites arrived at Mount Sinai. God descends in fire and thunder, and Moses receives the Ten Commandments, etched by the finger of God on stone tablets.

The mountain is described as being engulfed in smoke and fire, so intense that the people trembled at its base.

Is Mount Sinai Burned Rock or Volcanic?

Some believe the real Mount Sinai is not in Egypt but in Saudi Arabia, at a peak called Jebel al-Lawz. There, the top of the mountain appears blackened as if scorched by intense heat.

- Geologists are divided into:
- Some say it's natural volcanic rock or darkened by wind and sun
- Others believe it shows signs of high-temperature burning not typical of the region.

The Altar of the Golden Calf

Near Jebel al-Lawz, researchers claim to have found:

- A stone structure that could be an altar

- Ancient carvings of bulls or calves on nearby rocks, what was intriguing was the fact that the images of cows on those rocks, were the exact image of the drawings found of cows in Egypt.

According to the Book of Exodus, the Israelites made a golden calf idol at the foot of Mount Sinai while Moses was away. The discovery of bovine imagery adds intrigue—could this be the altar described in the Bible?

What Do Critics Say About the Exodus?

Skeptics point out that:

Ancient Egyptian records make no mention of Hebrew enslaved people or the Exodus.

- No large settlements or burial sites have been found in the Sinai from that era.

- Some scholars believe the story was written centuries later to unify the people of Israel under a shared national narrative.

Still, the absence of evidence is not necessarily the evidence of absence, especially when it comes to nomadic desert life thousands of years ago.

Faith in the Wilderness

Whether you believe the Exodus was literal history or a sacred metaphor, its meaning still speaks:

- Deliverance from bondage

- Trust in the unseen

- Receiving truth in the wilderness

- The journey from slavery to identity

Chapter Six

The Blood that Speaks

What if the blood of Jesus was not only found, but still alive

That's the claim made by Ron Wyatt, an amateur archaeologist who, in the early 1980s, claimed to have encountered one of the most incredible discoveries in biblical history. According to his account, he found not only the Ark of the Covenant but what he believed to be the very blood of Jesus Christ, dried on the mercy seat and later confirmed to contain a miraculous chromosome count.

It's a story that has inspired awe, devotion, and intense controversy. Could it be true? Or is it one of the greatest faith-based myths of the modern age?

The Discovery of the Ark and the Blood

On January 6th, 1982, Ron Wyatt claimed to have found the Ark of the Covenant in a cave beneath Golgotha—the site traditionally believed to be where Jesus was crucified. Inside the cave, he said, he saw a dried black substance that appeared to have spilled onto the top of the Ark's mercy seat.
Mysterious Artifacts - Mysteries Explored. https://mysteriesexplored.com/category/mysterious-artifacts/

When he returned with samples for testing, that black substance turned out to be blood.

But not just any blood.

According to Wyatt, the lab technicians in Israel found something that stunned them: the blood contained only 24 chromosomes.

- 23 chromosomes from the mother

- 1 Y chromosome

-

He was told, "This blood is alive." By a lab technician, and then asked. "who's blood is this?"

Wyatt interpreted this as divine proof: the Y chromosome indicated the child was male, but the absence of 23 paternal chromosomes meant there was no earthly father. For him, this was unmistakably the blood of Jesus—the Messiah—who was born of a virgin and conceived by God.

Live Blood?

Wyatt explained that dead blood cannot be thoroughly analyzed in terms of chromosomes—it loses many of its properties. However, by placing the sample in a body-temperature growth medium for 48 hours, the lab reportedly revived white blood cells, enabling a complete chromosome count.

"You can't get a chromosome count from dead blood," Wyatt explained. "But we got one from this. That means the blood was alive."

Connection to the Crucifixion

The most dramatic detail in Wyatt's story is the location: he claimed the Ark of the Covenant was buried directly beneath the site of Jesus' crucifixion. A crack in the rock—caused by an earthquake—allowed the blood to flow down through the earth and onto the mercy seat, fulfilling ancient symbolism in a literal way.

Wyatt said, "When the people who tested the blood asked, 'Whose blood is this?' I told them, through tears—'It's the blood of your Messiah.'"

An Earthquake in 33 A.D.?

Interestingly, a study published in International Geology Review confirms that a significant earthquake did occur in Jerusalem around 33 A.D., the year of Jesus' death, according to many biblical scholars. There was also a solar eclipse on the same day.

Researchers estimated it was a magnitude 6.0 quake, likely on April 3rd, 33 A.D.—the day many believe Jesus was crucified.

Could this be the quake that split the ground at Golgotha?

What Do Critics Say?

Ron Wyatt's claims have been widely criticized and dismissed by scholars, archaeologists, and even Christian researchers. Here's why:

- He never allowed independent experts to verify the location of the Ark or test the blood.

- His photographic evidence is unclear or missing.

- The Israeli government and mainstream labs have not confirmed his findings.

- Major archaeological organizations have not endorsed his work.

Even Wikipedia notes that "as far as we are aware, nothing was ever discovered to support his claims."

Critics argue that Wyatt's passionate storytelling and lack of peer-reviewed documentation make it impossible to accept his claims as historical facts.

Could It Be True?

Still, Wyatt's story won't go away. Videos of his testimony, lab reports, and lectures continue to circulate, especially among Christians who believe God has revealed evidence of the truth in the end times.

Whether you believe Ron Wyatt or not, his story invites deep reflection:

- Could God have left physical proof of Jesus' divine identity?

- Why would living blood be found thousands of years later, unless it was meant to be seen?

- What are we to make of the many confirmed elements—the earthquake, the ancient site, and the Ark's known connection to atonement?

Faith and the Mystery of Blood

The Bible says that "the life is in the blood" (Leviticus 17:11) and that Jesus' blood speaks "a better word than the blood of Abel" (Hebrews 12:24). Whether Wyatt's story is a miracle or a myth, the symbolic power remains:

- Blood atones

- Blood protects

- Blood connects heaven to earth

Chapter Seven

Science and the Bible

Conflicts and Resolutions

The Creation vs. Evolution Debate

The creation-evolution controversy has been a topic of debate for ages, and scientists, theologians, and the public have argued over it with great enthusiasm. The discussion is basically about the origin of life and the universe, and creationism takes the stand that a creator entity is responsible for the creation of all that lives, as witnessed in the Bible. On the contrary, the theory of evolution, supported by a host of empirical facts, contends that life emerged as a result of natural processes spanning millions of years. This inherent disagreement challenges the historical authenticity of the biblical record and the interpretation of scriptures from a scientific perspective.

One of the inherent aspects of this debate is how the Genesis account of creation is interpreted. Most adherents view this record as a literal historical account, but some argue that it could be a metaphorical or allegorical description of God's creativity. This is required, as it dictates how one balances faith and scientific facts. Archaeological findings have, at times, validated biblical accounts, and at other times, they have questioned the occurrence of some events. The issue is to identify what interpretations are acceptable both from a historical and a Christian faith perspective.

The scientific tradition emphasizes the importance of the scientific process and empirical facts in explaining the natural world. Fossils, genetics, and geology are all contributors to a model for describing the evolutionary process. These findings have led to the adoption of evolution by most scientists, yet the idea is still denied by certain religious denominations that grant authority to biblical scripture. The disagreement between science and faith reflects the usefulness of open discussion and civil discourse between the two opposing positions.

A second illustration is the biblical account of miracles, which also intersects in this case. Skeptics question the occurrence of miraculous happenings and regard them as myths or embellishments. But the believers would take such miracles as divine interventions for which room must be made within the framework of faith and history. This clash of perceptions accounts for the difficulty in reconciling miraculous occurrences with a scientific view of reality. These accounts must be dealt with with sensitivity and care for their historical and theological context.

Lastly, the creation vs. evolution debate requires one to examine more essential philosophical questions of existence, purpose, and what is truth. Examining archaeological evidence, scientific fact, and biblical scripture, a clearer picture can be discerned. Bridging this divide between these two extremes can result in a wiser discussion regarding the relationship between science and scripture, where an honorable dialogue respects both reason and faith. This is an ongoing conversation in seeking knowledge and wisdom in a world that is constantly changing.

Miracles and Natural Law: A Scientific Rejoinder

The subject of miracles and natural law has been debated for centuries, particularly when examining biblical events. Miracles have often been described as out-of-the-ordinary events that defy the laws of natural explanation. Miracles defy the scientific laws based on empirically observable and reproducible events. This does not necessarily mean that miracles cannot be present where there is scientific knowledge. Instead, this conversation promotes a more subtle discussion of why miracles can be explained within natural law rather than as naked exceptions thereto.

As time has passed, the great majority of the miraculous occurrences recorded in the Bible have been called into question regarding their authenticity. Archaeological findings have provided tremendous illumination of these records, generally verifying the facts that are consistent with historical models. For instance, archaeological excavations relating to the Exodus or the life of Jesus have triggered controversy over whether or not these records are factual. By using the historical and archaeological information, we can better appreciate the scientific and cultural environments in which these miracles were chronicled.

The scientific approach to examining miracles also calls for a re-examination of the definition of a miracle. Rather than presuming miracles to be falsehoods or exaggerations, they must be accepted as actions that were perhaps misconstrued or misrepresented in their original contexts. This opens the interpretive framework for invoking both the fallibility of human understanding and the possibility of divine intervention within the bounds of natural law.

Also, religion and science are connected in the sense that both of these disciplines try to explain the same reality, but from various perspectives. While science relies on empirical evidence, religion clings to the metaphysical. Such a duality is not necessarily conflictual but rather inviting of dialogue. Understanding that miracles, if at all, function within the bounds of natural law enables us to carve out a more harmonious relationship between scientific inquiry and religious faith.

In short, the issue is how to reconcile the concept of miracles with scientific law. Taking a scientific approach to biblical miracles, we can establish their historical authenticity with due regard for people's beliefs about them. Not only does such an analysis explain the nature of miracles, but it also sheds light on our understanding of science and scripture and, finally, enables us to have a better understanding of reality in general.

Chapter Eight

King or Prophet

Was Jesus just a wise teacher and prophet—or was He truly the Son of God? The Gospels portray a man who performed miracles, fulfilled prophecies, and challenged earthly powers. But how much of this story is supported by history, and how much is a matter of faith?

Let's take a closer look at some of the most well-known events in Jesus' life.

What Happened at the Birth of Jesus?

According to the Bible, Jesus was born in Bethlehem, fulfilling a prophecy from the Old Testament. Angels announced His birth to shepherds, and wise men from the East followed a star to bring gifts fit for a king.

Historical View: While many historians accept that Jesus was a real historical figure, the details of His birth—such as the star, the virgin birth, and the visit of the Magi—are not confirmed by any outside historical records. Some scholars believe that these elements were added to highlight Jesus' divine significance.

Why Did King Herod Kill All the Babies in Bethlehem?

Matthew's Gospel says Herod ordered the killing of all boys two years old and younger in Bethlehem to eliminate a rival, 'King of the Jews.'

Skeptical View: Although Herod was known for his brutality, including killing his family members, no Roman or Jewish historian of the time (like Josephus) mentions this specific massacre. Some believe the story may have been symbolic or exaggerated, meant to echo Pharaoh's actions in the time of Moses.

Did Jesus Turn Water Into Wine?

At a wedding in Cana, Jesus reportedly turned water into wine—His first public miracle, according to John 2:1–11.

Scientific/Skeptical Take: There is no external historical or scientific confirmation of this event. Critics suggest it could be metaphorical, representing transformation or abundance. Believers see it as a literal miracle that revealed Jesus' divine nature.

Is There Any Proof of This Miracle Outside the Bible?

There are no contemporary non-biblical records documenting this miracle. Early Christian writers refer to it, but only through secondhand tradition.

Scholarly View: Some argue that if such a public miracle had occurred, it might have been recorded in other ancient writings. Others believe that because Jesus' early ministry was largely local, it's not surprising that outside sources didn't record it.

Did Jesus Help Simon Catch Fish?

Luke's Gospel recounts that Simon (Peter) had caught nothing all night, until Jesus told him to cast his nets again, resulting in a miraculous haul.

Interpretation: Some see this story as a symbolic call to faith and discipleship rather than a literal miracle. Others accept it as a demonstration of Jesus' authority over nature.

Did Jesus Walk on Water?

The Gospels claim that Jesus walked across the Sea of Galilee during a storm to reach his disciples, calming the sea as he went.

Alternative Theories: A 2006 study proposed that rare weather conditions might create ice patches on the sea, possibly giving the illusion of walking on water. However, this theory is speculative and not widely accepted as a historical fact. The event has no documentation outside the Bible.

Did Jesus Heal the Soldier's Ear in the Garden of Gethsemane

When soldiers came to arrest Jesus, Peter cut off the ear of a servant named Malchus. According to Luke's Gospel, Jesus immediately healed the man.

Skeptical Analysis: This miracle is mentioned only in one Gospel and lacks any outside historical support. Some scholars see it as a literary or theological moment meant to emphasize Jesus' message of peace and forgiveness.

Final Thought

Whether you believe Jesus was a divine miracle worker, a mighty prophet, or a figure shaped by oral tradition and faith, there is no question that He changed the world. The stories of His life—revered by some, questioned by others—have endured for over 2,000 years. What you do with those stories is up to you.

Chapter Nine

Integrating Science and Faith

The Dialogue Between Scientists and Theologians

Many biblical events throughout history have been questioned from a scientific angle. Findings from archaeological excavations have provided explanations and support for some of the biblical accounts, breaking the old myth that science and religion cannot go together. For instance, archaeological discoveries regarding ancient cities mentioned in the Bible have stirred interest and controversy, as such evidence can either affirm or debunk historical records in history books.

The definition of miracles is another point of contention between the two disciplines. Scientists are still skeptical, demanding natural causes when miracles are being explained, while theologians perceive them as acts of intervention by God. This contradiction raises a further debate regarding what constitutes a miracle and whether exceptional events documented in religious texts are history-based or are, in reality, myths. There are some individuals who take the middle ground and believe that both are true. They believe that there is a God, but God sometimes can use natural means for miracles.

Also, the debate often goes on to explain scientific hypotheses and how they correlate with biblical beliefs. For instance, the theory of evolution has significantly challenged traditional interpretations of creation in the Bible. Nonetheless, scientists and theologians alike suggest bringing the two together, implying that evolution could be seen as a tool used by a divine creator rather than a competing narrative. Then there are people who believe that evolution is impossible, due to the fact that they see the primates as very similar yet with differences that cannot be reconciled.

Last but not least, the dialogue between religion and science is not just about settling arguments; it is about constructing respect and comprehension. Both, as they participate in open discussions, can enlighten one another on the mysteries of life and aid in establishing a better consciousness of reality. This rapport is the proof of symbiosis for science and religion to coexist, expanding the intellectual and spiritual facets of our lives.

The Role of Faith in Conceptualizing Scientific Findings

Science and faith have traditionally been polarized forces, but they can be compatible. The interaction of faith and scientific revelations results in a better understanding of both fields. Faith, for some, is an avenue through which scientific evidence can be interpreted, providing a way for people to transcend seeming inconsistencies between scripture and empirical data. In this chapter, how faith can add depth to scientific progress, specifically to knowledge regarding ancient biblical history and archaeological findings, is considered.

Ultimately, the dialogue between scientists and theologians is more about reconciling differences; it's about respecting and understanding one another. As they communicate freely, they can uncover the complexities of life and move forward with a broader horizon of reality. It reveals that science and religion can coexist, enriching the intellectual and spiritual aspects of our lives.

The Role of Faith in Understanding Scientific Discoveries

Religion and science have also been observed to be against one another, but they can coexist. The dance of religion and science suggests a greater appreciation of both. To many individuals, religion provides a framework through which scientific advancements are interpreted, which allows individuals to settle apparent contradictions between the Bible and empirical observations. This chapter discusses how religion promotes a greater appreciation of scientific advancements, in particular, of biblical accounts from ancient times and archaeological discoveries.

The historical accuracy of biblical incidents has been a topic of debate for both religious and non-religious people. Religion requires the believer to have faith in these incidents as part of a greater divine scheme. At the same time, scientific observation attempts to verify or falsify them based on archaeological and historical accounts. The double analysis thus allows us to understand history better, bringing to light multiple layers of meaning that are not necessarily clear at first glance. With every new archaeological find, religion tries to put these into perspective, explaining them in biblical records.

Religion is also significant when it comes to miracles in the Bible and believing and interpreting them. Skeptics may call them exaggerations, but to believers, they are solemn realities that convey God's work in the world. The question then becomes how to balance belief and skepticism so that one may be able to experience the miraculous without excluding a scientific cause. Such a discussion can lead to a greater understanding of the nature of miracles and their significance in religious and scientific domains.

Furthermore, the debate between science and faith encourages a spirit of cooperation. These scientists of strong religious backgrounds hold the belief that their work is worship, employing their knowledge of things to decipher the secrets of the world. Such an attitude provides an atmosphere in which religion and science merge, giving us results that lead us to visualize larger things in this world. If religious groups and scientists both adopt a cooperative stance, they can benefit from a greater pursuit of the truth.

Briefly, the role of religion in articulating scientific discovery is rich and complex. It challenges individuals to wrestle with the boundaries between their beliefs and the evidence presented by science. By being open to the possibility that science and religion are not conflicting, we can better appreciate the biblical events of the past, miracles, and archaeological finds that enable us to reconcile with the nuances of our humanity. Ultimately, the integration of these two disciplines will result in a deeper comprehension of the secrets of life and a closer distance between science and scripture.

Considering the case studies of the synchronization of science and scripture, we have thrilling accounts that demonstrate how biblical writings may be synchronized with archaeological and historical facts. One of the most excellent examples is the case of the excavation of Jericho, where archaeological excavations have questioned the biblical account of its destruction. Others think that the evidence is more consistent with the biblical account of walls suddenly collapsing, but others think that chronology suggests a slower decline. This ongoing controversy points to the necessity of rigorously examining both the biblical accounts and the archaeological evidence in hopes of understanding the past more clearly. Another excellent case study would be accounts of the ancient civilizations spoken about in the Bible, such as the Hittites.

Once thought to be mythical, archaeological excavations in modern-day Turkey have proved that such a civilization did, indeed, exist, thus providing historical validity to the accounts provided within the Bible. By revealing the reality of the Hittites through artifacts and inscriptions, one can do justice to the complexity and richness of the biblical story and its connection to real historical events and thereby create the scope for how archaeology can serve as a bridge between reason and religion. The miracles themselves, as presented in the Bible, are another scope where harmonization is interesting.

For instance, the Red Sea parting account has been scientifically questioned, with scientists proposing natural explanations, e.g., tidal activity or volcanic activity. These explanations do not reduce the miraculous nature of the event for Christians but, instead, provide windows for dialogue between scientific explanation and theological account. If one examines these miracles from a scientific perspective, then people can appreciate both their religious significance as well as their history. The Dead Sea Scrolls provide another example of the intersection of archaeology, history, and scripture.

They were uncovered in the middle of the 20th century and have since provided scholars with an excellent view of the world of the Bible and its scripture. They not only confirm the literary merit of the Old Testament, but they also give the context in which these authors lived. The Scrolls establish the age-old nature of these writings and how applicable they remain in religious and scholarly communities, indicating how these documents might harmonize historical discoveries with what the Bible affirms about them. Overall, the harmonization case studies reveal a sophisticated but complex relationship between religion and science.

Through scientific examination of biblical accounts, historical records, and archaeological data, we can form a more detailed image of what is presented in the biblical accounts. Such harmonization creates a mutual respect dialogue for science inquiry and religion and, therefore, facilitates deeper insight into the truth in the scriptures. Through these case studies, we can witness how the pursuit of knowledge can deepen and not diminish our understanding of the divine.

The discovery of the Fibonacci code dates back to the 13th century, when Italian mathematician Leonardo of Pisa, known as Fibonacci, introduced a simple numerical sequence in his book Liber Abaci. He used it to solve a problem about rabbit population growth, not realizing he had uncovered a mathematical pattern found throughout nature. The Fibonacci sequence—where each number is the sum of the two before it—appears in pinecones, seashells, sunflowers, and even galaxies, revealing a hidden order in the chaos of the natural world.

One could argue that the existence of the Fibonacci sequence could prove the existence of a creator. Possibly a scientific creator?

Chapter Ten

The Death of Jesus

The crucifixion of Jesus is one of the most pivotal and emotionally charged events in all of Christian history. For believers, it's the moment of ultimate sacrifice. For historians and skeptics, it's a documented Roman execution surrounded by religious symbolism and political tension. This chapter explores what we know—biblically, historically, and scientifically—about Jesus' final hours.

The Crowd Picked Barabbas Over Jesus

According to the Gospels, during Passover, it was customary for the Roman governor to release a prisoner. Pontius Pilate offered the crowd a choice: Jesus or a known criminal named Barabbas. The crowd chose Barabbas.

Biblical View: All four Gospels describe this choice, portraying Jesus as the innocent one rejected by the people He came to save.

Historical View: There is no Roman documentation confirming this specific Passover custom; however, some historians believe it's plausible, as Roman officials sometimes employed gestures of appeasement to maintain peace in volatile provinces like Judea. However, some scholars argue that the Barabbas story may have been used to shift blame from Rome to the Jewish people.

What Is Crucifixion Like?

Crucifixion was a violent form of execution used by the Romans for criminals and rebels. Victims were typically nailed or tied to a wooden cross and left to die slowly from suffocation, blood loss, and exhaustion.

Medical Perspective: Doctors and forensic researchers say that death by crucifixion would likely involve dislocated shoulders, nerve damage, muscle cramps, and slow asphyxiation. A 1986 article in the Journal of the American Medical Association detailed how Jesus likely experienced excruciating pain consistent with the known effects of crucifixion.

How Heavy Were Crosses in Jerusalem During the Time of Christ?

Historical and archaeological evidence suggests that the entire cross (both upright and crossbeam) may have weighed over 300 pounds. However, it's believed that victims often carried only the crossbeam (patibulum), which weighed around 75–125 pounds. January 29 | Bioethics Ireland. https://bioethicsireland.ie/bible/bibeth/january/jan29/

Biblical Note: The Gospels mention that Jesus was too weak to carry His cross the entire way, so a man named Simon of Cyrene was forced to help.

Why Did They Pierce the Side of the Dead on the Cross?

According to John 19:34, a Roman soldier pierced Jesus' side with a spear, and blood and water flowed out.

Medical Interpretation: Modern forensic analysis suggests that the 'blood and water' could represent the separation of blood components after death, supporting the idea that Jesus was already dead when pierced. This would also ensure no one survived the execution, which was standard Roman practice.

Historical Insight: Romans commonly broke the legs of crucified victims to speed up death. In Jesus' case, since He had already appeared to be dead, the spear ensured it.

They Gave Jesus Vinegar Instead of Water

The Gospels record that when Jesus said, "I thirst," He was offered a sponge soaked in sour wine (vinegar) on a hyssop stick.

Cultural Note: Sour wine (or posca) was a typical drink among Roman soldiers, not a form of torture but more likely a readily available liquid. The offering may have fulfilled Psalm 69:21: "They gave me vinegar for my thirst."

What Did Jesus Say on the Cross?

The Gospels record several statements, including:

- "Father, forgive them, for they know not what they do." (Luke 23:34)

- "Today you will be with me in paradise." (Luke 23:43)

- "My God, my God, why have you forsaken me?" (Matthew 27:46, quoting Psalm 22)

- "It is finished." (John 19:30)

Each saying reflects different theological messages—suffering, forgiveness, fulfillment of prophecy, and divine purpose.

What Did Jesus Say When He Died?

According to Luke, His final words were, "Father, into your hands I commit my spirit." (Luke 23:46)

This echoes Psalm 31:5 and indicates a voluntary surrender, even in the face of death.

Is There Any Documentation of Jesus' Crucifixion Besides the Bible?

Yes, though not extensive.

Tacitus, a Roman historian writing around 116 AD, mentioned that Pontius Pilate executed Jesus during the reign of Tiberius.

- Josephus, a Jewish historian, referenced Jesus' crucifixion in Antiquities of the Jews (with some debate over Christian editing).

- Lucian of Samosata, a Greek satirist, mocked Christians for worshiping a man who was crucified in Palestine.

Scholarly View: While details differ and external records are sparse, the crucifixion of Jesus is one of the most historically accepted facts about His life, even among secular scholars.

Who Was Responsible for Having Jesus Crucified?

Biblically, it was a collaboration between Jewish religious leaders and Roman authority. The Sanhedrin accused Jesus of blasphemy, while Rome executed the charge of claiming to be "King of the Jews."

Historical Context: Rome reserved the right to execute, so while religious leaders played a role, only Roman officials had the power to crucify. Some scholars believe the Gospel writers may have downplayed Roman involvement to avoid conflict with Roman readers in the early Church.

Final Thought

The crucifixion of Jesus stands at the crossroads of faith, history, and politics. Whether you see it as the ultimate sacrifice for humanity or as the tragic execution of a Jewish teacher, it remains a defining event in world history. The cross has become a symbol of hope to billions, and a reminder of how one life ended brutally, which continues to shape the world centuries later.

Chapter Eleven

Was There a Ressurection

The resurrection of Jesus is the cornerstone of the Christian faith—without it, the claims of divinity and eternal life lose their foundation. But did it happen? This chapter explores burial customs, relics, ancient letters, and scientific investigation to examine the evidence for and against the resurrection of Jesus.

What Were the Tombs Like in the Days of Jesus?

During the time of Jesus, tombs in Judea were typically rock-cut chambers. Wealthier families often used family tombs carved into limestone hillsides. Bodies were laid on stone benches, and after a year, the bones were collected into an ossuary (bone box).

Biblical accounts state that Jesus was buried in a borrowed tomb owned by Joseph of Arimathea, fulfilling a prophecy that he would be 'with the rich in His death.'

How Much Did the Stone on Jesus' Grave Weigh?

Archaeologists suggest that the stones used to seal tombs in 1st-century Judea were large and disk-shaped, weighing between 1 and 2 tons. It would have taken several men to move one of them.

The Gospels describe the stone as being 'rolled away'—and notably, the women who visited the tomb wondered who would help them move it, reinforcing the idea that it was not something that could be easily displaced.

What Is the Shroud of Turin?

The Shroud of Turin is a long linen cloth bearing the faint image of a man who appears to have been crucified. Many believe it to be the burial cloth of Jesus. Shroud Of Turin - ImagineInkjet. https://imagineinkjet.com/shroud-of-turin/

It is housed in the Cathedral of Saint John the Baptist in Turin, Italy, and has been revered by some and questioned by others for centuries.

What Does Science Say About the Shroud of Turin?

Carbon dating tests in 1988 dated the cloth to the Middle Ages (around 1260–1390 AD), suggesting it may be a medieval forgery. However, critics of the test argue that the sample was taken from a portion of the cloth that had been repaired, potentially skewing the results.

More recent studies have analyzed pollen, bloodstains, and textile patterns, some of which are consistent with 1st-century Middle Eastern burial practices. As of today, science has neither definitively proven nor disproven the authenticity of the Shroud.

"The Shroud of Turin: Evidence of Radiation Beyond Modern Capability"

Scientific analysis of the Shroud of Turin has revealed that the image possesses unique properties not found in any known artwork or natural process. The image behaves like a photographic negative and contains three-dimensional spatial information, detectable through image-processing techniques like the VP-8 Image Analyzer—something no painting or scorch mark has ever demonstrated. Notably, the image is confined to the outermost linen fibers, just a few microns thick, with no penetration to deeper layers, and no known pigment, dye, or brushstroke is present. Some scientists, including those in the Shroud of Turin Research Project (STURP), have suggested the image may have been formed by a burst of high-energy radiation, possibly ultraviolet or even an unknown form, due to the precision and superficial nature of the markings. According to experts like Giulio Fanti and Paolo Di Lazzaro, duplicating the image would require radiation levels far beyond modern technological capabilities, leading to speculation that the image's formation involved phenomena beyond current scientific understanding even of today.

What Were Jewish Customs Surrounding the Burial Cloth?

Jewish burial customs in the first century involved wrapping the body in linen cloths, often with a separate face covering. Spices and ointments were used to prepare the body, and burial typically occurred quickly, within 24 hours of death.

This aligns with Gospel descriptions of Jesus being wrapped in a shroud and buried before sundown on the day of His crucifixion.

A Letter Written by Pontius Pilate Regarding Jesus' Death and Gravesite

Several apocryphal texts claim to include letters written by Pontius Pilate to Roman officials about Jesus' trial, crucifixion, and burial. One such document, 'The Report of Pilate to Tiberius,' describes Jesus' miracles and final moments in dramatic detail.

While interesting, these documents are not included in official Roman archives and are considered pseudepigraphical—likely written centuries later by Christians to support their beliefs.

A Letter from Pontius Pilate Interviewing Mary and Joseph

Some documents claim Pilate met with Mary and Joseph or their relatives. These letters appear in various medieval texts, but historians widely agree they are fictional, written long after the events they claim to describe.

There is no historical evidence that Pilate ever personally interviewed Mary or Joseph.

What Was the Crown of Thorns Made Of?

The Gospels mention that Roman soldiers placed a crown of thorns on Jesus' head as a form of mockery. Scholars believe it may have been made from the jujube plant (Ziziphus spina-christi), common in the region and known for its long, sharp thorns.

No physical artifact has been confirmed as the original crown, though several cathedrals claim to possess pieces of it.

Where Were the Letters from Pontius Pilate Stored?

Ancient Christian writings claim that Pilate's reports were sent to Rome and stored in the imperial archives. However, no such official documents have been found in Roman records. Most surviving 'Pilate letters' come from medieval texts or apocryphal Christian writings.

The lack of documentation has led scholars to classify these letters as religious literature rather than historical evidence.

What Does Science Tell Us About the Letters from Pontius Pilate?

Modern historians and textual critics have examined these letters and found linguistic styles, cultural references, and theological content that point to later authorship, usually between the 3rd and 6th centuries AD.

While they offer insight into early Christian beliefs and attempts to defend the faith, they are not considered credible historical documents from the Roman Empire.

Final Thought

The resurrection of Jesus remains one of the most debated events in history. Faith holds it as the triumph over death. Skepticism asks for proof. In between are relics, traditions, and ancient writings—some mysterious, some miraculous, and some artificial. Whether literal or symbolic, the story of the resurrection continues to inspire belief, provoke debate, and raise timeless questions about life after death.

Chapter Twelve

The Nephilim and the Kandahar Giant

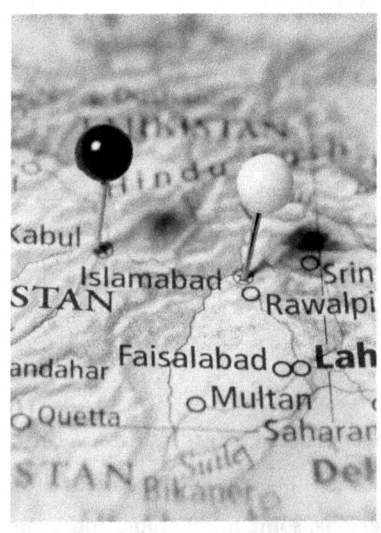

In 2002, a highly trained tactical team known to be well-respected Marines allegedly encountered and killed the Kandahar Giant, who was described as measuring 13 feet tall with bright red hair, six fingers on each hand, and two rows of teeth.

https://allthatsinteresting.com/kandahar-giant

A defense contractor by the name of Mr. K reported that he saw this incident happen while on duty for Operation Enduring Freedom, where the giant killed one Special Forces trooper before being dispatched by continuous rounds of fire.

The legend began when a group of troops was reported missing on patrol in Kandahar's mountains. An investigating team, made up of special operatives studying the disappearance, stumbled upon a cave where they discovered the giant. The soldiers engaged the creature in a firefight, and it was killed in the process. The government reportedly recovered the giant's body, and the soldiers involved were compelled to sign confidentiality agreements.

Despite the government's refutations and lack of evidence, conspiracy theories still circulate regarding the Kandahar Giant. Some believe that the government is keeping something secret, while others believe the story is a result of biblical prophecy. However, some biblical scholars understand the stories of the Nephilim, in which the giant is a product of, as metaphors rather than historical accounts.

Moreover, there is no concrete evidence to prove the existence of the Kandahar Giant. The tale is in the mouths of soldiers who passed through Kandahar in 2002, but the story is questionable.

In the Bible, 'Nephilim' is referred to in the Book of Genesis, Genesis 6:1-4. The passage reads like this:

"When human beings started multiplying on the earth and giving birth to daughters for them, the sons of God saw that the daughters of human beings were beautiful, and they took any of them they wanted in marriage. Then the Lord said, 'My Spirit will no longer try to contend with humans, for they are mortal; their days will be numbered at a hundred and twenty years.'"

"The Nephilim were on earth in those times—and also later—when the sons of God had intercourse with the daughters of man, and they bore children to them. They were men of note, heroes of old."

The term 'Nephilim' is disputed as regards interpretation and argumentation among scholars and theologians. Others believe that the Nephilim were the offspring of a union between the 'sons of God' and the 'daughters of men.' The 'sons of God' are disputed and are interpreted by some as being fallen angels or celestial beings.

The Nephilim are described as being 'heroes of old, men of renown,' which suggests that they were men of great power or standing in the past. The Bible otherwise does not provide much data on the Nephilim or their role in human history.

Interpretations of Nephilim vary between religious and cultural traditions. Some interpret them as angels or giants, and others see them as symbolic figures representing themes such as the fall of man or punishment for disobedience.

Overall, the biblical account of the Nephilim in Genesis is one of fascination and contention, and their specific nature and import are still topics of contention among scholars and believers.

Other Biblical References to the Nephilim:

Numbers 13:32-33

[32] And they spread among the Israelites a bad report about the land they had explored. They said, "The land we explored devours those living in it. All the people we saw there are of great size. [33] We saw the Nephilim there (the descendants of Anak come from the Nephilim). We seemed like grasshoppers in our own eyes, and we looked the same to them."

Current Day Sightings

There have been numerous sightings of giant-like beings on the planet, particularly in mountain regions. Several people have purported to have taken photographs of them, with at least one reportedly going missing after posting such content on YouTube. This has fueled conspiracy theories that the government is actively suppressing the facts.

What Do the Critics Say?

The adversaries of the Nephilim concept approach the topic in theological, historical, and scientific contexts. Popular arguments include:

Mainstream archaeology rejects proof of giant human fossils despite multi-year assertions and anecdotal claims. Believers say they have been suppressed or ignored, while skeptics cite hoaxes, misidentifications, or exaggerations.

- Biblical references to Nephilim are few and vague. Dramatically varying interpretations have been made, and some classify them as symbols or myths.

- Science points out that there is no confirmation. There is no authenticated evidence of 'giant people' in any world museum or university.

- Massive cultural myths, movies, and internet rumors have fueled modern conceptions of giants, and it is hard to separate fact from folklore.

- Others focus on critical thinking and caution that unsubstantiated claims are being sold without evidence to back them up.

Final Thoughts

Although many testimonies and eyewitness reports—just like the case of UFOs—there is no evidence that the Nephilim and the Kandahar Giant exist. With little evidence and many differing accounts, it is still one of those things that everyone needs to interpret for themselves.

Chapter Thirteen

Ascension

The story doesn't end at the resurrection. According to Christian belief, Jesus appeared to His disciples, gave final instructions, and ascended into heaven. But what did He say, what did He leave behind, and how does science approach the supernatural claims that followed? This chapter explores those questions and more.

How Long Did the 11 Disciples Claim That Jesus Stayed on Earth After His Resurrection?

According to Acts 1:3, Jesus appeared to His disciples over 40 days after His resurrection, speaking to them about the Kingdom of God. These appearances included personal conversations, shared meals, and final teachings.

Skeptics often argue that these post-resurrection appearances could have been visionary experiences, emotional responses to grief, or the result of oral tradition developing over time.

What Was the Message of Good News That Jesus Left With His Disciples?

The core message Jesus left was the 'Good News' or Gospel: that He had died for the sins of humanity, had risen from the dead, and that through faith in Him, people could have eternal life. He instructed His followers to share this message with the world (Matthew 28:19–20).

This message became the foundation of Christianity, rapidly spreading through the Roman Empire in the decades following His death.

What Did Jesus Claim He Left Behind With Them So They Could Work Miracles?

Jesus promised His disciples that the Holy Spirit would come upon them, empowering them to perform miracles, speak in new tongues, and spread the Gospel boldly. Acts 2 describes the arrival of the Holy Spirit on the day of Pentecost, an event that launched the early Christian Church.

Believers view this as a supernatural fulfillment of Jesus' promise; skeptics, on the other hand, see it as part of the theological narrative developed by early followers of Jesus.

What Does Science Say About the Miracle of Healing?

Studies have explored the role of belief, prayer, and community support in the healing process. Some clinical trials have shown small benefits from intercessory prayer, while others have shown no significant effect. The placebo effect—where a person improves simply because they believe they are being treated—also plays an important role.

Most scientists conclude that while faith can influence psychological and physiological health, there's no definitive proof of supernatural healing through prayer alone.

What Does Science Say About Prophecy?

Science generally explains prophecy through psychology, probability, and the phenomenon of confirmation bias. People often interpret vague or symbolic predictions as if they were fulfilled events, especially in hindsight.

That said, some prophetic claims in religious texts remain debated, particularly those that appear to be specific. Critics argue these may have been written after the events or edited over time.

Are Near-Death Experiences Scientifically Proven?

Near-death experiences (NDEs) are reported by people who have come close to death and describe vivid sensations, such as seeing a light, meeting deceased relatives, or feeling peace.
The Mystery of Near-Death Experiences: - ndeinsights.info. https://ndeinsights.info/the-mystery-of-near-death-experiences/

Neuroscientists suggest that NDEs are likely caused by brain activity during trauma or a lack of oxygen. However, some cases remain difficult to explain, especially when people report events they could not have seen or heard during unconsciousness.

While not proof of an afterlife, NDEs continue to intrigue both scientists and spiritual seekers.

Where Do the Dead Claim to Have Gone When They Die?

During a routine orthopedic surgery, a 12-year-old boy under general anesthesia experienced something no one could explain. Though his body lay unconscious on the operating table, he later described floating above it, watching the doctors work. He recalled vivid details: the precise arrangement of instruments, snippets of conversation, and the rhythm of the monitors beeping below. Then, suddenly, he was surrounded by a tunnel of brilliant light and filled with an overwhelming sense of peace. There were no visions of angels or departed relatives—just a powerful stillness and a knowing that he was somewhere beyond the physical world. When he awoke, the surgical team was stunned by his account. He had been fully anesthetized, without measurable awareness, yet what he described matched reality too closely to ignore. His experience, documented in a medical journal, would become one of the first scientifically recorded near-death experiences in a child under anesthesia, raising profound questions about the nature of consciousness and what might lie beyond the veil of life.

Those who report near-death experiences often describe places of light, peace, or encounters with spiritual beings. Some describe realms resembling heaven or other concepts of the afterlife from their culture or religion.

Skeptics argue these are brain-generated experiences influenced by belief, while others see them as potential glimpses of life beyond death.

Doing a YouTube search, you can find near-death experiences in hell", you will find an extensive amount of people who claimed to have gone to hell after a near-death experience. Every experience is not duplicated, but they all adhere to many similarities.

Final Thought

The ascension of Jesus and His final instructions continue to shape the faith of millions. Whether one sees the promised miracles and spiritual encounters as divine truth or psychological phenomena, they remain powerful testaments to the human longing for meaning, connection, and hope beyond this life.

Chapter Fourteen

Conclusion: A Path Forward

Embracing Complexity in Faith and Science

The intersection of science and faith tends to be an area full of complexity, where each domain seeks to understand in its own terms. Accepting the complexity gives one the possibility to examine the intricacies of biblical accounts together with scientific findings.

Biblical events: Historical accuracy can sometimes be questioned. However, the majority of scholars believe that those accounts have profound verities that strike a chord universally in human experiences regardless of empirical acceptability. By embracing the richness of these controversies, we invite new meanings and interpretations.

Science and the Bible are viewed as adversaries, but a closer inspection reveals chances of reconciliation. For instance, reports of scientific phenomena elaborated in the scriptures could be read in a manner respecting their past time frame. Miracles narrated in religious texts may initially appear to be overstatements, but they can be interpreted as reports of human experiences rather than facts. This makes it possible to consider deeply what it is to witness and document extraordinary occurrences.

Archaeological evidence, as it applies to biblical references, again adds to this conversation, presenting physical proof that can affirm or disprove established interpretations. The revelation of ancient relics and inscriptions assists in shedding light on the surrounding history of biblical happenings, thereby deepening our knowledge of their meaning. This evidence leads to queries regarding the constitution of truth as it exists both in science and scripture, challenging us to examine how evidence forms our beliefs and conceptions.

Embracing complexity involves welcoming conflicting opinions and acknowledging that science and faith each have their part to play in our understanding of the world. This crossroads can be used to find a fuller, more insightful worldview that appreciates empirical facts and individual faith. It opens the door to conversations beyond too-simple dualities, enabling a more holistic study of knowledge that honors both the scientific and the spiritual.

Ultimately, this odyssey of questing for the intersection of faith and science encourages another level of interaction with the mysteries of existence. As we navigate this multifaceted terrain, we develop a deeper appreciation of the stories that compose our convictions and the facts that compose our knowledge regarding them. By making room for change that honors both disciplines, perhaps we can construct an even greater narrative that offers room for the diversity of human experience in all its forms.

Encouraging Open-Mindedness and Debate

Encouraging open-mindedness and debate is required in addressing the intersection of science and scripture. In today's world, where historical factuality and scientific evidence tend to collide with traditional beliefs, the establishment of a platform on which individuals can feel free to present alternative views is crucial. Open-mindedness allows for further examination of biblical events and the scientific principles that oppose or confirm them. Through the cultivation of this attitude, we are better able to appreciate the refinement of both reason and faith.

Dialogue is a bridge between conflicting positions, enabling constructive discussion of archaeological finds and meanings relative to biblical records. When individuals dialogue respectfully, they can share perceptions and findings that otherwise may be unappreciated. Dialogue of perspectives not only grows understanding but also provokes participants to rthink their stance based on new data. The aim is not to establish victory but to seek truth through collaborative inquiry.

In reflecting on miracles described in the Bible, open-mindedness is a necessary tool for distinguishing fact from hyperbole. In being open to examining various explanations of miracles, individuals can find multiple meanings that enrich the scientific study and religious belief. This thought can lead to a greater clarity of the cultural and historical context behind the stories, as well as their long-lasting impact on religious groups.

Promoting discussion also entails addressing cynicism that generally accompanies arguments about science and religion. People are usually connected to their own beliefs, and this evokes defensiveness that stunts positive discussion. By being open-minded, we can accommodate questions and different opinions. This openness not only accumulates knowledge but also fosters belonging among those seeking to balance their religion with scientific studies.

Lastly, knowledge-seeking entails being dedicated to openness and debate. As we navigate the complexities of biblical accounts and scientific exploration, we must remain open to hearing other voices. This not only enriches our knowledge of the interplay of science and scripture but also fosters a culture of respect and inquiry, which benefits all areas of study, from archaeology to theology.

Looking to the Future: Science, Scripture, and Humanity

When we look to the future, science and scripture come together both as a challenge and an opportunity for humankind. These two domains have been at war with one another throughout our history, with scientific discoveries at times opposing biblical truths. When scrutinized more closely, however, most of the so-called conflicts result from misunderstanding or misreading scientific data and also scriptural writings. This ongoing discourse provokes an examination of how such disciplines can coexist and assist us in knowing the universe and our place in it better.

Archaeological findings in recent times have shown that biblical events have firm evidence backing them up, hence making some scriptural narratives plausible. Archaeological digs in regions outlined in the Bible brought to light places and artifacts corresponding to conventional accounts, thus disproving that such narratives are mere fantasies. Such discoveries not only verify the aspects of biblical history but also lead to further investigation of the contexts under which the events occurred, providing a more nuanced appreciation of the scriptures as historical accounts.

For another, the documentation of miracles presents an intriguing case for study. While skeptics would typically denounce miraculous occurrences as fictitious, a closer inspection reveals that numerous different viewpoints can indeed explain such phenomena. Scientific inquiry can shed light on the psychological and sociological forces that give rise to perceptions of miracles without ruling out divine action. This dualism allows for a civil discourse between believers and skeptics as each searches for truth together.

Exploring the subtleties of these arguments, one must emphasize the role of faith within an understanding of science and scripture. Faith is capable of providing a frame through which individuals interpret scientific evidence and history, giving an outlook that corroborates and enlightens their knowledge. By establishing an environment in which questioning and doubt are fostered, we can create a culture where empirical evidence and divinely ordained wisdom are valued equally, ultimately arriving at a fuller interpretation of man's life.

The challenge in the future will be to bridge the gap between scientific knowledge and scriptural interpretation. Interdisciplinary collaboration between scientists, theologians, and historians is called for in addressing concerns raised at this point. Collectively, as they speak with each other, these disciplines are capable of developing a dialogue that not only strives to resolve conflicts but rejoices in the celebration of the tapestry of life, ushering us into an age where science and scripture collaborate to make our world more affluent, not poorer.

CONCLUSION

Throughout this book, we've traveled from Genesis to giants, from miracles to modern mysteries. We've examined the Bible's most iconic stories—creation, the flood, the life of Jesus, His death and resurrection—side by side with what history, archaeology, and science have to say.

We've asked tough questions:

- Did the universe begin with a Creator or a cosmic bang?

- Were biblical miracles acts of God, or legends told to inspire belief?

- Is there objective evidence for giants, prophecy, or life after death?

- And most importantly, is the Bible a book of truth... or just another fairytale?

Some readers may walk away from this book with renewed faith, seeing divine fingerprints behind history and human experience. Others may come away with more profound questions, holding firmly to skepticism, science, or reason. And some may land right in the middle, living with mystery and wonder.

And that's okay.

The point of this book was never to give you my answer; it was to provide you with both sides, open the conversation, and invite you to think for yourself.

Whether you believe the Bible is the literal word of God, an ancient moral guide, or a blend of truth and myth, it's undeniable that it has shaped the world like no other book in history.

So now, as you close these pages, the final question still stands:

Truth... or fairytale?

You decide

References

B ecause this book is written for a general audience and blends biblical topics, modern mysteries, and scientific critique, your references will be a mix of:

- Biblical scripture
- Historical sources
- Scientific and skeptical works
- Apologetic and theological perspectives
- Popular topics (e.g., Nephilim, Shroud of Turin, Kandahar Giant)

Further Reading and References

Biblical Texts

- **The Holy Bible (Genesis, Exodus, Psalms, Gospels, Acts, Revelation)**

Historical and Religious Scholars

- **The Bible Unearthed – Israel Finkelstein & Neil Asher Silberman**
- **Jesus: Apocalyptic Prophet of the New Millennium – Bart D. Ehrman**
- **Jesus and the Eyewitnesses – Richard Bauckham**
- **The Historical Jesus – John Dominic Crossan**
- **The Case for Christ – Lee Strobel**
- **Evidence That Demands a Verdict – Josh McDowell**

Scientific & Skeptical Perspectives

- **Misquoting Jesus – Bart D. Ehrman**
- **Why People Believe Weird Things – Michael Shermer**
- **The Demon-Haunted World – Carl Sagan (for scientific thinking and skepticism)**

Archaeology & Ancient Texts

- Josephus, Antiquities of the Jews

- Tacitus, Annals (mention of Jesus' crucifixion)

- Apocryphal and pseudepigraphal writings (e.g., Letter of Pilate to Tiberius)

Topics on the Shroud of Turin

- The Shroud of Turin: The Burial Cloth of Jesus Christ? – Ian Wilson

- Peer-reviewed studies (e.g., Radiocarbon Dating of the Shroud of Turin, Nature, 1989)

- Pollen and textile research from Max Frei and Giulio Fanti

Modern Legends and Mythology

- Reports and interviews about the Kandahar Giant (various online/conspiracy sources—use discernment)

- Analysis of giant skeleton claims and Smithsonian conspiracy theories (Snopes, National Geographic commentary)

Biblical & Theological Interpretations of the Nephilim

- Reversing Hermon – Dr. Michael Heiser
- Giants, Sons of the Gods – Douglas Van Dorn
- Various theological commentaries on Genesis 6 (e.g., NIV Study Bible, ESV Study Bible)

www.ingramcontent.com/pod-product-compliance
Lightning Source LLC
Chambersburg PA
CBHW071236090426
42736CB00014B/3110